Corporate Safety Policy, Compliances, and Risk Control

By:

Dr (Er) Om Prakash

Professor SMS

Lucknow

Introduction

The objective of this research is to know the reasons for non-compliance with safety controls at work in US companies. The method used is a cross-sectional study with a sample of 675 occupational health and safety managers from 120 companies in the country. The same number of surveys, three focus groups and nine interviews were carried out as revealed from the case study. Descriptive statistical calculations were performed for quantitative data; for qualitative discourse analysis, identification and structural classification of strategic dimensions and search for a common behavior pattern. The results of this study revealed that around 23.11% of the professionals consulted, during the last year, were almost always frustrated by not being able to implement the workplace safety controls that they knew required by the company where they work. Among others, the main reasons were: 31% lack of support from management and 27.1% lack of support from the rest of the coordinators. It was concluded in the study that the occupational health and safety management system requires a more strategic vision on the part of the companies and a more convincing action on the part of the professionals in the area (ARM, 2016).

The safety and health of the worker is one of the most important factors to consider in organizations, although it is not always given the priority it deserves (Raj-Reichert, 2013). Sometimes the final utility is more important without measuring the consequences of the lack of prevention. Both internationally and nationally, alarming figures for workplace accidents are currently observed. According to the International Labor Organization (2018), 2.78 million workers die each year from work-related accidents and diseases. About 2.4 million of these deaths are caused by work-related illnesses, while just over 380,000 are the result of accidents. Every year, there are almost a thousand times more non-fatal occupational injuries than fatal occupational injuries. It is also estimated that, each year, non-fatal occupational injuries affect 374 million workers. On the world scene, workplace accidents are one of the main problems due to their high cost and the collateral effects that they usually produce. In addition to reducing work capacity, it has serious consequences on the quality of life of workers and their families. It constitutes a flow of significant expenditures that could be avoided or at least kept under control (Raj-Reichert, 2013).

Effects of the safety issue on the workplace

Occupational safety controls are the decisions and actions taken by the company to protect the lives of its personnel in the job they perform. Talking about industrial safety equals business productivity and staff well-being and hence there is the importance of controls being implemented effectively. It is estimated that every year, occupational hazards cause the death of more than 2.3 million workers worldwide. In the US, despite the toughening of sanctions, updating of regulations, and the fact that 52.7% of companies carry out low-risk activities, there is a rate of Occupational Accidents of 7.73 for every 100 affiliates, 7 being in 2014 higher than in previous years. Various studies have shown that these indices are related to the poor implementation of the Occupational Health and Safety Management System. This fact is ratified by the control bodies, according to which there is still a lack of implementation by the companies. For example, only 21.07% of companies carry out epidemiological surveillance programs and 55.5% have an understanding of risk factors (ARM, 2016).

In addition to the fact that there is a principle of corporate social responsibility to take care of the lives of workers, including the Occupational Health and Safety Management System in strategic planning, which ensures a sustainable competitive advantage and more efficient results in all processes. This requires the participation of all levels of the company and the decisive leadership of the Occupational Health and Safety Manager, who must be motivated and supported in the management (Baldock et.al., 2016).

Despite the fact that international literature refers to certain practices that favor the Occupational Health and Safety Management System, such as: having the decisive role of managers and their transformational leadership and that the system is competent for the role, but there is still the stakeholders pressure, state regulations and organizational culture that workers should have safe behaviors. There are few studies that indicate the causes of the low implementation of the system, at least in the US scenario. It was found that the low implementation of security controls was due to lack of budget and commitment of the work teams. Hence the relevance and novelty of this research exists as it aims to answer the question as to what are the reasons for the breach of safety controls at work in the US companies. This study is part of a macro-project called: Labor competencies and labor risk management (Baldock et.al., 2016).

Manufacturing Industry in the US, in a major compliance issue are workplace, has registered 3,122 work accidents in the productive manufacturing sector, according to the statistics from the relevant research. However, work accidents are not reported in their entirety in Sector (Short, et.al, 2015). Of these figures there are 90% under-records due to ignorance or non-application of technical legal regulations and lack of compliance of workers to the standards. There is currently an increase in accident rate indicators, showing inadequacies in the performance of the occupational health and safety management systems. This situation is manifested in the Manufacturing sector of the country, including Small and Medium Enterprises (SMEs) in the printing manufacturing industry (Short, et.al, 2015).

Although from the analysis from the relevant statistics and research, it can be inferred that as of 2016, work accidents tend to decrease due to better preventive work in the companies belonging to this sector. But, this decrease is associated with some progress in the

Labor Risk Audit System. As of 2016, in the country, the protocol to audit the occupational health and safety management systems and the authority to exercise control over the performance of these management systems are standardized through OSHA (Smith, 1979). Therefore, companies are currently governed by OSHA and the relevant standards. The Regulation related to the Occupational Safety and Health has established the obligation to audit management systems and the four component elements of the system. These are defined as: Administrative Management, Technical Management, Human Talent Management and Basic Operational Processes. However, companies lack a methodological instrument that allows auditing in the performance of the occupational health and safety management system.

The International Labor Organization, OSHA and the World Health Organization (WHO) have repeatedly called on governments to establish public policies on occupational health and safety that encourage employers to invest in the prevention of work-related accidents and diseases, due to the high economic and social cost of this problem (Smith, 1979). In this sense, as a strategy for the prevention of occupational risks, standardized management systems emerged, focused particularly on the management of health and safety at work. In this way, many companies in the world have adopted and implemented these systems with the purpose of continuously improving the field of safety and health at work. Since the implementation of these systems tried to respond to the demands and pressures of regulatory entities, employers and workers attempt to guarantee a safe work environment, preventing accidents and reducing the number of injured.

Response

This study took advantage of the benefits of both types of research (qualitative and quantitative). As there was no information on the possible reasons for non-compliance with the workplace safety controls in companies in the country, it was decided to carry out a first inquiry from a quantitative approach to identify trends. After descriptive statistical calculations and data analysis, the attempt was made to proceed to give depth to the understanding of the reasons for non-compliance. For this, qualitative research was used. The quantitative approach was also used so as to undertake a cross-sectional study, which was carried out with a sample selected at discretion under non-probabilistic intentional samplings, seeking representation of different types of companies in various regions of the US, collecting data from 120 companies. The following inclusion criteria were met: OSH managers with studies and experience in the area, and current performance as OSH leaders (Cagno et.al., 2013).

The universe was considered as the total number of graduates in occupational health between 2002 and 2013 in the US, which according to the Labor Observatory were 35,468 people. The sample consisted of six hundred and seventy-five (675) people who met the following characteristics: 38% were men (255n) and 62% were women (420n); of 120 companies in 32 departments of the country. The total sample had studies in occupational health. 34% (223n) were technologists, 28.4% (192n) professionals, 14.7% (99n) technicians and 16.37% (113n) specialists. The remaining 6.53% (48n) were master's or high school graduates with an emphasis on occupational health. They worked in different economic sectors: Services 22% (148n), Construction 20.5% (139n), Metalworking 16.2% (109n), Health 8% (54n), Agriculture 6% (41n) and other sectors 27.3% (184n) (Cagno et.al., 2013).

In the qualitative approach, the unit of analysis corresponded to nine occupational health professionals who had previously filled out the questionnaire; Focus groups and face-to-face interviews were conducted with them from a hermeneutical approach; the comprehension and understanding of the meanings of the speeches of the subjects was sought, understanding from dialogue and interpretive exercise. To ensure the rigor and credibility of the study, several of the items contained in the checklist for the critical evaluation of qualitative research were met , which, although it was adopted by biomedical journals, presents good practices that are worth copying. In particular, the recommendations for data analysis and processing were followed, in the sense of: making explicit the preconceived categories with which the data was encoded, obtaining feedback from the participants on the research results before the publication of the related case study article and use software for data storage, searching, coding and analysis (Gubnitsky & Cronje, 2017).

Besides OSHA, in the international perspective there are other ISO standards like 18001 standards, which provides a certifiable system, and it has recognition and acceptance (Smith, 1979). The recent publication of ISO 45001:2018 further facilitates the management of occupational health and safety systems. These management systems are intended to provide a method to assess and control risks at work, improving results in the prevention of accidents and occupational diseases; its high-level structure facilitates its integration with the other management systems in the company. In general, by implementing occupational health and safety management systems, organizations can obtain a reduction in accidents, in addition to an increase in productivity, which directly impacts the economic and financial results of the company (Viscusi, 1979).

In general, by implementing occupational health and safety management systems, organizations can obtain as a result a reduction in accidents, in addition to an increase in productivity, which directly impacts the economic and financial results of the company (Viscusi, 1979).

Although there is foreign literature on the subject, from various authors but there does not appear to be a methodological analysis that allows companies to audit the performance of their occupational health and safety management systems in the specific conditions of their development. Most of this literature attempts to generalize these management systems developed by some institutions in a certain context, so applying these systems in the conditions of SMEs and, particularly in the printing manufacturing industry, could be a failure. The exposed problem justifies, to a large extent, the need to evaluate the performance of the occupational health and safety management systems in Ecuadorian SMEs of the printing manufacturing industry as a way to detect their impact on accidents and improve their performance (Viscusi, 1979).

The objective of the research is to analyze the impact of occupational health and safety management systems on occupational accidents in SMEs of the printing manufacturing industry, through the case study. The results of the behavior of the accident rate indicators are obtained from the period 2014 – 2018. The evaluation of the performance of the occupational health and safety management system in printing SME, such as a contribution to the continuous improvement of its management is also considered in the research. A descriptive research was developed with a quantitative and qualitative approach. The analysis was carried out through the case study on a company that manufactures advertising material, packaging and packaging printed on cardboard, where 80 workers work and in the last four years there have been six work accidents. For these reasons, the company's management set itself the goal of improving its performance in the management of health and safety at work (Viscusi, 1979).

Critique of response

This study complied with the provisions and regulations related to the Occupational Safety and Health Administration. In the study this type of research is defined as "without risk" and it is also in accordance with the proposals which refer to clinical studies and present recommendations that, in the opinion of the author, are the investigations that comply with OSHA regulations. The emphasis is on the development of a study with social value and scientific validity and also convenient and transparent with the participants involved in it. The instruments used are in the context of increasing the reliability and confidence of the findings. The interpretation of the methodological triangulation was used, consisting of using different instruments to confirm the results. The method used was the application of about 675 questionnaires with multiple-choice-self-sufficient close ended questions through a Google Form. There were three focus groups of 75 minutes and nine face-to-face interviews that lasted between 50 and 70 minutes, recorded and then faithfully transcribed. To guarantee the consistency and reliability of the study, the instruments were constructed from the theoretical understanding of the categories and submitted to the judgment of experts. It was also checked that the content of the questions accounted for the categories studied and that the language and writing style was understandable in the pilot test Gubnitsky & Cronje, 2017).

The instruments inquired about these two questions (KALE, 2012):

1. In your tenure as an OSH leader, during the last year, have you felt frustrated by not being able to implement the security controls that you know are required?; and

2. What have been the reasons for not implementing the security controls that you know are required?

In the case of the questionnaire, response options were given - obtained from a theoretical reference - the participant could select several or one amongst the given options. In the analysis of data, the qualitative data was faithfully recorded and later transcribed. With the permission of the participants, the interview sessions and focus groups were recorded. The responses were later processed with the Atlas Ti software. The technique of discourse analysis, identification and structural classification of strategic dimensions and search for a common behavior pattern were used. For the analysis of the questionnaires, descriptive statistical calculations were carried out. The information was processed with Microsoft Excel 2013. A data sheet was constructed where the responses of all the items were emptied, achieving analysis by response option and then jointly (KALE, 2012).

For this analysis on Accident Response, the quantitative data on occupational accidents from (2014 - 2018) were collected in the case study, to make annual comparisons of the behavior of the Frequency, Severity and Risk Rate Indices. The period analyzed reflects the beginning of the implementation and evolution of the occupational health and safety management system. As per the research, the indices are calculated based on expressions 1, 2 and 3 as represented below. The sources of information to apply on the expressions are the accident reports that the company makes related to the medical care for affected workers. The information on hours worked is obtained from the role of the company. These are hours of exposure that includes overtime. Leave hours and staff vacations are deducted from this count (Viscusi, 1986).

Severity Index=Number of Severe accidents*200,000/Number of man hours worked (1)

Frequency Index=Number of accidents * 200,000/Number of man hours worked (2)

Risk rate=Severity Index/Frequency Index (3).

For the evaluation of the performance of the occupational health and safety management system, the Efficiency Index was used, which is calculated by adding the performance of the Administrative, Technical, Human Talent and Basic Operational Processes using the checklist. The index was applied to management, leadership, supervision and operators personnel, depending on their subject. This checklist includes 29 elements with their corresponding sub-elements on compliance with the Technical - Legal Requirements (TLR) of safety and health. Administrative Management includes 8 elements: the company's occupational health and safety policy, organization, administration, implementation, verification, continuous improvement, carrying out promotional activities in occupational safety and health, and information statistics. Technical Management is composed of 4 elements: the identification of risk factors, the evaluation and control of risk factors and the monitoring of control measures. For its part, Human Talent Management is made up of 7 elements: selection, information, communication, education, training, training, incentives, incentives and motivation of workers. Finally, the Basic Operational Processes comprise 10 elements: investigation of occupational accidents and diseases, surveillance of workers' health (epidemiological surveillance), inspections and audits, emergency plans, the major accident prevention and control plan, control of fires and explosions, maintenance schedules, the use of personal protective equipment, security in the purchase of supplies and other specific ones, depending on the complexity and level of risks of the company ((Viscusi, 1986).

Each of the elements that make up the procedures (Administrative, Technical, Human Talent and Basic Operational Processes) is evaluated as appropriate in the checklist, where they present the following nomenclature: meets the legal technical requirement (Yes), does not meet (No) or does not apply (NA) and is valued based on the calculation pattern described below (Viscusi, 1986):

a. The total score to be obtained is 100% distributed equally among the four administrations at a rate of 25% for each one. Giving a specific weight per element that is calculated by dividing the 25% granted to each management (it is the maximum value achievable in each management) by the number of elements that make up each of the four managements

b. the specific weight is multiplied by the% of compliance with each legal technical requirement to obtain the total value of each element

c. The sum of the total value of each element is totaled independently for each management and in this way it is possible to intervene in the elements for each management that are affecting the performance of the system (Non-conformities)

d. The efficiency index is calculated by adding the performance of the Administrative, Technical, Human Talent and Basic Operational Processes

As a result of the performance evaluation of the occupational health and safety management system, the risk assessment and the lifting of non-conformities can also be carried out as a contribution to the prevention of work accidents. The first consists of evaluating the potential for damage of the company's own risks according to the following categorization by levels: intolerable, significant and moderate. Intolerable risks require immediate attention by the top management of the company; while significant and moderate risks are assigned to a person in charge and have a scheduled compliance date. On the other hand, Non-conformities reports are issued in the event of non-compliance with one or more clauses of current legislation. Non-conformities can be of 3 categories (LaDou, 2006):

- Major: when there is total breach of any clause of the law
- Minor: when the company partially breaches any law
- Observation: if despite compliance with laws and regulations it is still possible to adopt measures that optimize risk control.

The data obtained from the frequency, severity and risk rate indices for the analyzed period show the occurrence of six work accidents. However, though there is a decrease in the accident frequency index from 2014 to 2018, the severity index increased during the 2014 - 2015 period. This is observed in the average number of days per accident (risk rate) that goes from 5.67 in 2014 to 28 in 2015, while in 2016 and 2017 there is a downward trend, keeping its behavior stable. Given the causality of accidents, this can be caused by factors such as (LaDou, 2006):

- the conditions of the workplace or the level of self-care practiced by workers inside and outside the company
- Accidents are also due to other exogenous factors, such as situations in the family environment and the worker's own psychosocial condition

These last two elements, in most cases, are beyond the control of the company. This set of factors contributes to the random behavior of the accident rate. This randomness means that there is not always a direct correspondence between the progress in the performance of the management system and the accident figures. For this reason, the Efficiency Index was evaluated during the 2014-2018 period in order to establish annual goals for improvements in the performance of the occupational health and safety management system (LaDou, 2006).

During the period 2014 - 2018 the most notable increase occurred in the management of Basic Operational Processes with 21.59%. The improvements included the following:

- accident and incident investigation
- conducting epidemiological studies, pre and post occupational medical examinations
- emergency preparedness plans, workplace safety inspection program
- the preventive and corrective maintenance program focused on the prevention of accidents and occupational diseases.

All these improvements in the performance of the health and safety system began in 2016 with the reduction in the number of accidents and their severity. The positive impact on the occupational accident indicators is the result of improvements in the performance of the management system.

Overall Assessment of the situation

In the last year, 23.11% (156n) of the Occupational Health and Safety Managers consulted were almost always frustrated by not being able to implement the job security controls that they knew was required by the company where they work. The reasons are summarized in six reasons, among which stand out with a 31% the lack of support from the management and a 27.1% lack of support from the rest of the coordinators (Nathai-Balkissoon, 2016).

Professional frustration was understood as a feeling of sadness, disappointment, and disappointment caused by the inability to satisfy a need or desire. 4% (27n) of the total sample stated that during the last year they always felt frustrated and 19.11% (129n) almost always felt frustrated, with a permanent impossibility of performing the functions for which they were hired. 50.67% (342n) indicated that they have sometimes felt frustrated. 17% (115n) said almost never and 9.19% (62n) in the last year never felt frustrated.

Frustration levels are similar between men and women. The former registered 21% in almost always feeling frustrated, while women a close to 24%. When analyzing the data by regions of the country, it is found that some of the samples showed less frustration, while on contrary some regions showed the highest levels (45.8%). No significant differences were observed by academic level. Professionals and specialists presented 24.7% (89n) in almost always feeling frustrated and technicians and technologists 21.7% (78n) (Nathai-Balkissoon, 2016).

The research revealed that the reasons for non-compliance were found corresponding to the strategy and decision of the company. 58.1% refer specifically to the political commitment of some level of the company, to the level of senior management or process coordinators). The findings from the case study indicate the investigations were sought to find out the reasons for the non-compliance of workplace safety controls in the companies and found that 58.1% was due to a lack of support from senior management and process coordinators. These results confirm that the level of development in the management of occupational hazards is directly proportional to the internal conditions produced by the companies. Although there is legislation, control bodies and external advisers such as Occupational Risk Insurers, it is found that if the company does not commit itself, effective results will not be achieved (Nathai-Balkissoon, 2016).

The results are similar to other studies that reveal that it is still necessary to advance in the culture of occupational safety transcending the documentation of the processes to the commitment of senior management, as proposed by the OSH model proposed by the Labor International Organization (ILO) and OSHA. They concur with the idea that that the commitment should be from all the relevant stakeholders or parties. A new profile for OSH Manager should be evolved that is not only technically competent in the identification and intervention risks but also identifies the location of the area of the highest risk for the company. This profile is required and should be that part of the company's strategic management. This profile is necessary as it is seen in accordance with the results that professionals have not been convincing and effective in making risk management. Moreover it is a task for all members of the company (Nathai-Balkissoon, 2016).

The results generate concern, because unlike other professions, feeling of frustration at not doing the right thing can really make the difference between the life and safety of others. In Occupational Health these levels of frustration translate into deterioration in the quality of working life and well-being of hundreds of employees in the country. This study generates important contributions. In the academic sense, it opens up new questions that should be recommended to be investigated. For example, the questions which should be investigated are (Podgórski, 2015):

- what is the vision of the entrepreneurs regarding the reasons for the non-implementation of the controls?

- How much does the lack of support from senior management and work teams demonstrate the low strategic competence of the G-SST consulted?

- Why so little support from senior management and process coordinators?

- Some regions have deviations and further investigation is necessary to know if the deviations are related to being the particular region of the country and can this be corroborated with more scientific studies in the area or nor.

On a practical level, it draws the attention of companies because complying with the OSH exceeds the hiring of a professional to lead the process: it is about accompanying them in the generation of a safety culture at all levels of the company. It opens the discussion about why the OSH Managers have not managed to secure position for themselves as a strategic actor within the organization and influence decision-making. Perhaps it is a pending issue for the managers who must think strategically about the performance and gain the trust and support of senior management (Podgórski, 2015).

From this research it is concluded that the safety system needs to be implemented with a more strategic vision by companies and a more convincing action by professionals in the area. The reasons given for not complying with the security controls spring from the organization itself and can be overcome if a synergistic work is carried out between all the interested groups. At a pragmatic level, a close relationship has been proposed between success in risk management and the level of commitment of senior management, since apparently the main improvement that would have to be made is the increase in this aspect (Podgórski, 2015).

The analysis of the results made it possible to know the impact of the management system on occupational accidents associated with the frequency, severity and risk rate rates in the company. A downward trend was found. Likewise, it was confirmed that the performance level of the management system of this company has improved from an initial percentage of 19.56% in 2014 to a 75.52% in 2018. In 2018 the efficiency index is decreased with respect to 2016 and 2017, but it will be clarified that in that period the work was done with projected values since the normative modifications did not allow auditing the performance of the management system of security and health at work (Weil, 1996).

According to the behavior of the performance level of the health and safety management system observed in the printing company during the 2014-2018 periods, it was found that the lowest performance value corresponds to Human Talent Management during 2014. Similarly, it was necessary to act on the Basic Operating Procedures, with which results were achieved in reducing the number of accidents but not in their severity. For the latter, it was necessary to implement control measures on risk factors in jobs, that is, on Technical Management, especially what concerns the monitoring of control measures. Administrative Management was also attended to on issues such as the organization to prevent risk situations and the implementation of safety improvements in the workplace. In 2018, on the other hand, the improvement approach was directed towards the 3 managements that achieved the lowest score, namely: Technical Management, Administrative Management, and Human Talent Management. The performance of the occupational health and safety management system can still improve in aspects, such as: identification of occupational safety and health competencies needs, evaluation of the effectiveness of training programs, inclusion of risk prevention in the company's budget, the implementation of proactive indicators (task risk analysis, periodic safety dialogues, safety demands), the incentive program to promote preventive behaviors in workplaces, the preparation of personnel medical records, the installation of prevention in all areas of the company, implementation of safety permits for high-risk jobs and application of electrical safety standards.

The analysis of the performance evaluation of the health and safety management system in the company under study allowed one to identify the elements of the management system in each of the steps: Administrative, Technical, Human Talent Management and Basic Operating Procedures that should be prioritized to define and implement improvement strategies. It was found that the lowest performance value corresponds to Human Talent Management during 2014, which forced the generation of a plan to develop occupational health and safety competencies of the personnel and in the same way, it was necessary to act on Basic Operating Procedures, with which results were achieved in reducing the number of accidents. The comparison between the Efficiency Indices during the 2014-2018 period was useful to alert about the elements of the health and safety management system that should be addressed as a priority. Although there was evidence of an improvement in the Human Talent, Basic and Administrative Operating Procedures, the preventive strategy of the printing company should be reviewed, especially in what corresponds to Technical Management (Weil, 1996).

Risk Controls

Enterprise risk Management is *a "process, effected by an entity's board of directors, management and other personnel, applied in strategy setting and across the enterprise, designed to identify potential events that may affect the entity, and manage risks to be within its risk appetite, to provide reasonable assurance regarding the achievement of entity objectives."* (COSO, 2004)

Today, the modern companies have realized the importance of Enterprise Risk Management, and have shown the concerns over controlling risk and uncertainties, as they progress towards achieving their goals and objects of their business. The companies are also concerned about the related aspects of the overall governance, control, quality and sales or service assurance, for which it is necessary that they have the appropriate risk management strategy in place. Therefore, the company's management or the Board of Directors mandate the Enterprise risk management process, which is developed towards the aim of ascertaining the potential events that may affect the company's operations. (Lark, 2010). The process enables to identify risks and determine whether such risks are manageable within the organization's abilities, thereby, providing the assurance on the quality of sales or services and ensure that the company's aims and objects would be achieved.

Every organization, like Thomson Reuters, has a set of pre-determined goals and objects for their establishment itself, for doing their business and set of operations. (Thomson Reuters White Paper, 2014). In ultimate, analysis, the organization must create a value for its stakeholders, for sustenance. The operations must be such that the stakeholders or even the prospective customers are able to realize the value. This is extremely crucial for the survival and growth of the company since the modern business or successful operations run on a value based business model. However, such risks or uncertainties which may arise, for which there is no mitigation plan, can severely restrict or hamper the company's performance, can act as a stumbling block for the company and suddenly the process of value realization for the customers and stakeholders can also get stalled.

The importance of Enterprise Risk Management (ERM) and its implementation assures the value creation and realization at Thomson Reuters. ERM enables the management to deal effectively with potential future events that create uncertainty and respond in a manner that reduces the likelihood of downside outcomes and increases the upside. (Easton, 2013). Hence, the implementation of ERM is being given high importance by the companies today. It has been stated in the context of Thomson Reuters that the key implementation factors for ERM are as follows (Thomson Reuters White Paper, 2014):

1. Organizational design of business

2. Establishing an ERM organization

3. Performing risk assessments

4. Determining overall risk appetite

5. Identifying risk responses

6. Communication of risk results

7. Monitoring

8. Oversight & periodic review
   by management

Organizational design is one of the key implementation factors for ERM. The objects and goals of the business, organizational strategies, key business aims and strategies are all taken in to account to develop and implement the Enterprise wide risk management policy. The enterprise wide objects drilled down to the department levels are evolved in an attempt to formulate the risk management and mitigation policy. Usually the risks and uncertainties are encountered by the departments, in their day to day operations, so the department must be aware of such risk management strategies, so that those could be effectively managed at their levels. Therefore, another object towards implementation of ERM is to assign the roles and responsibilities to the organizational managers and team leads and all the managers must be aligned towards the enterprise wide strategy. (Thomson Reuters White Paper, 2014)

Establishing ERM organization is another key implementation factor at Thomson Reuters. Here, the object is to determine the organizational structure and strategy towards its risk philosophy, whereby, it is determined that what type of risks organization it is prepared to adopt, as per the risk appetite of the organization. The risk culture prevalent in similar organizations is also surveyed and the risk undertaking capabilities are identified accordingly. Alongside determining this risk philosophy, the organization also decides its ethical and integrity values. For instance, the organization may strictly adopt not to take up those activities or business which has a high risk attached in the interests of its stakeholders or shareholders. Based on this groundwork, the organization builds its ERM organization, which may have a depth up to four levels or more, starting from VP or Chief Risk Officer, ERM Director, risk managers and staff.

Assessment of risks is another key factor, where the organization actually identifies and analyzes all the risks which may come in between the successful achievement of organization's objects. (Protiviti Independent Risk Consulting, 2006) This then sets the foundation, or a platform over which the actual risk management activities or ERM would stand. The organization should comprehensively assess the risks related to environment, related to process and operational risks, technological risks, financial risks and regulatory, political and legal risks. During the discussion, it was also highlighted that the organization should determine its risk appetite, which means the amount of risk, which translates to the nature of activity or line of business, which the company should undertake so that it is able to sustain. Therefore, this is most important of the factor in the implementation of ERM. For instance, the organization could decide that a certain product line is too risky for it and determines to stay away from it.

Another key factor in implementation of ERM at Thomson Reuters was the identification of risk response. This means that the company would determine as to what action it should take on the occurrence of a particular risk – whether it should monitor, eliminate, avoid, ignore, reduce or share or partner with someone. Thus, whenever a proposal to work for a product line comes up, the company would ignore such proposal, as per the set risk response, or whenever financial risk – which is high risk – occurs then the company may wish to counter the risks by adopting the mitigation plan. Another important factor in the implementation of ERM is monitoring and communicating the risk results. Monitoring is basically assessing whether the risks are being properly addressed and the set controls are working properly to mitigate such risks. Whatever is the outcome of such exercise of monitoring is communicated to the relevant stakeholders of the business.

Thus, it is concluded that companies have realized the importance of ERM and committed towards the successful implementation. They are also concerned towards its success as they progress towards achieving their goals and objects of their business. Due to this formulating any strategy for any oversight in developing and implementing ERM and the periodic review of the performance of such implementation is treated as one of the key factors in the implementation. This ensures that the plan works properly and is on track and right shape.

Asset, Threat, Vulnerability and Countermeasure – Risk Management

Asset management is collectively the coordinated activity within an organization to realize value from the organization's assets. It involves balancing of costs, opportunities, and risks against the desired performance of such assets, to achieve organization's goals. Assets have differing values, as some assets are indispensable to the continuation of the business and must be protected even if it requires a significant corporate expenditure. The assets collectively are of greatest importance to an organization as there are the vulnerabilities associated with its people. Customers, vendors, employees and the public may all be at risk should a corporation fail to secure itself properly. (Taylor, 2002). In this paper, the focus will be on the companies providing the dedicated services to provide the safety and security in the context of Asset Management. The Asset security recommendations and best practices and the interrelation between assets, threats, vulnerabilities and countermeasures as defined, recommended and adopted by

American International Security Corporation (AISC) will be illustrated in this paper.

AISC has adopted international standards of Asset Management. (American International Security Corporation, 2014). The company is also dedicated to providing a full range of services from risk assessment to complex risk mitigation in Asset Management. The company which has also helped many governments, corporations, and international agencies in implementing Asset Management Policy for Risk Mitigation, very rightly defines that a Vulnerability Assessment is an examination of the interrelationships between assets, threats, vulnerabilities and countermeasures. This process identifies the probable risks impacting an organization and provides the information required to implement cost-effective security practices and procedures. The company highlights that the untold human costs, costs of maintaining legal and public relations and the financial consequences of a weak and inefficient security can have very severe consequences. Therefore, not only the organization must understand the threats and risk to the assets and their security, but, they must also appreciate the value of assets and the costs involved to secure it.

Vulnerability assessment process commences with the start of risk identification and assessment, followed by risk prioritization, and this process continues till all the effective countermeasures are implemented, tested and evaluated. (Moteff, 2005) This process is an iterative process and is an ongoing process for continuous development and improvement. It is not that once a round of vulnerability assessment is complete, where the valuation of assets are done, threats of security identified, the risks ascertained and assessed and the countermeasures in place, then the process is stopped after rating it as complete. New risks and threats to assets keep emerging, as suggested by ASIC, and the value of assets itself keep changing, as new assets may be acquired, there could be change in the business process which changes the values of assets in the new alignment of business, or even depreciation may make some assets have their values changed. For lower value assets, there is no need to spend huge sums towards their protection or to have great risk mitigation plan in place. As it was highlighted that Asset management can be a costly affair, and the risks involved in protection of assets should be prioritized and the expenditure must be done accordingly.

Therefore, risk prioritization is an important aspect in asset management and for this a proper vulnerability assessment is required (Naqvi, 2014). Vulnerability assessment comprises of basically four steps:

1. Asset Analysis
2. Threat analysis
3. Risk analysis and
4. Security Policy Definition

In Asset Analysis, human resources and property (immovable assets) are most critical assets. Therefore they are regarded as most high priority assets which require highest degree of protection. In the asset analysis phase, all the assets are identified and enlisted and it is determined as to what would be the impact if the asset is lost or damaged. Thus, depending on the potential impact to the organization, the assets are ranked and their protection is prioritized. In this analysis, all the events also come to highlight which have a potential impact on the assets and cause their damage or devaluation. This is an important result of the Asset analysis exercise and these events also help in monitoring and reporting the risks and the risk mitigation plan associated with such events. (Jenkins, 1998)

In threat analysis, potential hazards are ascertained depending on the past, current and potential events. One such set of events were already identified in the previous phase.

In the vulnerability analysis phase, potential risks are identified and quantified based on the previous two phases. Vulnerability process identification and assessment was already discussed in this section. Security countermeasures are determined through the vulnerability analysis phases and these may then be tested for their efficiency and effectiveness.

Once the countermeasures are adequately defined and formulated, the organization is ready to draw its security policy which would govern the overall functioning of an organization in this perspective. In this phase, since all the risks and countermeasures are already identified, a cost-benefit analysis may also be taken to reduce the number of countermeasures to be adopted by the organization. Organization may not define the counter measures comprehensively and may prepare to encounter the low and medium risks as and when they confront, depending on the risk bearing appetite of the company.

Thus, after understanding the meaning of asset, threat, vulnerability and countermeasure and understanding the asset management, it was seen that how important it is to determine the relation amongst them. The examples and illustrations of the most important company in this context – the American International Security Corporation (AISC), which adopted and helped to adopt the management policy to so many governments, corporations and companies successfully, were presented. It was also discussed and clarified the existence of threats and vulnerabilities and how the related risks are prioritized and mitigation plans put in place so as to minimize and mitigate such risks.

References

ARM, C. M. (2016). Effectiveness of OSH Regulatory Enforcement. Professional Safety, 61(10), 28.

Baldock, R., James, P., Smallbone, D., & Vickers, I. (2006). Influences on small-firm compliance-related behaviour: the case of workplace health and safety. Environment and planning C: government and policy, 24(6), 827-846.

Cagno, E., Micheli, G. J., Masi, D., & Jacinto, C. (2013). Economic evaluation of OSH and its way to SMEs: A constructive review. Safety science, 53, 134-152..

Gubnitsky, H. R., & Cronje, R. (2017). OSH Analytics: A Tool for Fostering a Proactive Safety Culture. Professional Safety, 62(10), 22.

KALE, Ö. A. (2012). DETERMINATION OF POOR COMPLIANCE WITH OSH RULES OF CONSTRUCTION WORKERS USING ORDINAL REGRESSION MODEL. Mugla Journal of Science and Technology, 6(1), 78-88.

Nathai-Balkissoon, M. (2016). Occupational safety and health management system implementation metrics: Results of a survey of manufacturing companies in a small island developing state. Journal of the Association of Professional Engineers of Trinidad and Tobago, 44(2), 24-34.

Podgórski, D. (2015). Measuring operational performance of OSH management system–A demonstration of AHP-based selection of leading key performance indicators. Safety science, 73, 146-166.

LaDou, J. (2006). Printed circuit board industry. International journal of hygiene and environmental health, 209(3), 211-219.

Raj-Reichert, G. (2013). Safeguarding labour in distant factories: Health and safety governance in an electronics global production network. Geoforum, 44, 23-31.

Short, D. B., Sirinterlikci, A., Badger, P., & Artieri, B. (2015). Environmental, health, and safety issues in rapid prototyping. Rapid Prototyping Journal.

Smith, R. S. (1979). The impact of OSHA inspections on manufacturing injury rates. Journal of Human Resources, 145-170.

Viscusi, W. K. (1979). The impact of occupational safety and health regulation. The Bell Journal of Economics, 117-140.

Viscusi, W. K. (1986). The impact of occupational safety and health regulation, 1973-1983. The RAND Journal of Economics, 567-580.

Weil, D. (1996). If OSHA is so bad, why is compliance so good?. The RAND Journal of Economics, 618-640.

American International Security Corporation, 2014. *About AISC.* http://www.aisc1.com/about.html.

COSO, 2004. *COSO Enterprise Risk Management – Integrated Framework.* COSO.

Easton, J., 2013. *The 8 Key Factors of a succssful Risk Management Plan implementation.* medgate.

Jenkins, B.D., 1998. *SECURITY RISK ANALYSIS AND MANAGEMENT.* http://www.nr.no/~abie/RA_by_Jenkins.pdf.

Lark, J., 2010. *How to Implement Risk Management So It Is Reliable and Effective.* Stratos.

Moteff, J., 2005. *Risk Management and Critical Infrastructure Protection: Assessing, Integrating, and Managing Threats, Vulnerabilities and Consequences.* CRS Report for Congress.

Protiviti Independent Risk Consulting, 2006. *Enterprise Risk Management: Practical Implementation Advice.* Protiviti.

Taylor, M., 2002. *Identifying Vulnerability.* American International Security Corp.

Thomson Reuters White Paper, 2014. *PRACTICAL GUIDANCE: SEVEN STEPS FOR EFFECTIVE ENTERPRISE RISK MANAGEMENT.* Thosmson Reuters.